WHAT MAKES PORNOGRAPHY "SEXY"?

WHAT MAKES PORNOGRAPHY "SEXY"?

John Stoltenberg

Milkweed Editions
Thistle Series

Except for brief quotations in critical articles or reviews, no part of this book may be reproduced in any manner without prior written permission from the publisher: Milkweed Editions, 430 First Avenue North, Suite 400, Minneapolis, MN 55401 Published 1994 by Milkweed Editions. Printed in the United States of America. Book design by Don Leeper. The text of this book is set in Adobe Garamond.

94 95 96 97 98   5 4 3 2 1

Milkweed Editions is a not-for-profit publisher. We gratefully acknowledge support from the Dayton Hudson Foundation for Dayton's and Target Stores; Ecolab Foundation; General Mills Foundation; Honeywell Foundation; Jerome Foundation; John S. and James L. Knight Foundation; The McKnight Foundation; Andrew W. Mellon Foundation; Minnesota State Arts Board through an appropriation by the Minnesota State Legislature; Musser Fund; Challenge and Literature Programs of the National Endowment for the Arts; I. A. O'Shaughnessy Foundation; Piper Jaffray Companies, Inc.; The St. Paul; Star Tribune/Cowles Media Foundation; Surdna Foundation; James R. Thorpe Foundation; Unity Avenue Foundation; Lila Wallace-Reader's Digest Literary Publishers Marketing Development Program, funded through a grant to the Council of Literary Magazines and Presses; and generous individuals.

Library of Congress Cataloging-in-Publication Data

Stoltenberg, John.
    What makes pornography "sexy"? / John Stoltenberg.
      p.   cm.
    ISBN 1-57131-201-3
    1. Pornography—Social aspects—United States.   2. Men—United States—Attitudes.   I. Title.
    HQ472.U6S863   1994
    363.4'7—dc20   94-3812
                                                            CIP

This book is printed on acid-free paper.

Dedicated to
the worldwide human-rights movement seeking justice and a voice
for victims of the sex industry.

And with special thanks to
the members of Men Against Pornography
who generously contributed ideas and leadership
to The Pose Workshop.

What Makes Pornography "Sexy"?

What makes pornography "sexy" to men? What is it about the pictorials in *Penthouse, Playboy,* and *Hustler* that makes men sexually aroused?

Before there was take-home pornography for VCRs, before there was interactive pornography on CD-ROM, there were magazines—called "men's sophisticates" by the publishing industry but more accurately "stroke books" in slang. Millions of copies are printed in the United States monthly; millions are exported; there are dozens of foreign editions; there are thousands of titles, each featuring scores to hundreds of individual photos; and thereby millions of men worldwide look at billions of photographs of women each year in nude or nearly nude poses intended to help each consumer feel sexually aroused "like a real man." That's what the pictures are supposed to *do.* If they did not do that, they would not be for sale.

But what are the pictures in those magazines really *of*? And why do those particular pictures produce that result?

What is it that men see when they look at pornography? Why do so many men keep looking, again and again?

Why do so many men feel an ongoing "need" for pornography in their lives? Why do men get "hooked" on pornography, becoming dependent on it for sexual arousal?

Can men learn to look at those pictures in such a way that they see what's really there, what's really happening to the human being in the photograph?

Can men learn to look at their own sexual relationship to pornography—and can men examine that relationship in a way that makes real change possible?

Can men learn to perceive how they perceive pornography? And if so, can men learn to perceive pornography differently?

More than ten years ago I decided to bring together a group of men in New York City to try to answer those questions. This is the story of what happened—and what I found out.

I first invited about a dozen men to attend a special showing of a slide show being offered by Women Against Pornography. In a cramped storefront office just off Times Square, we watched slide after horrific slide. At one point the voice-over said, "Try to imagine men in these poses." Those words stuck in my mind, somewhere below conscious awareness. In later years they were to unlock the "sexiness" of pornography for perhaps hundreds of thousands of men.

Immediately after the slide show, we were taken on WAP's tour of nearby pornography stores and live sex shows. I remember feeling numb. I remember being unable to talk to anyone I was with. And I remember that the other men in our small group seemed introspective and silent too. *How was this tourist trek through the urban sex industry going to help us find a way to talk about our experience of pornography?* I wondered to myself. *The very experience of watching that slide show and traipsing from sex show to loop booth was shutting us down inside.*

My activism against pornography began in 1976, when a movie called *Snuff* opened at a first-run theater in Times Square. Posters suddenly plastered throughout the New York City subway system showed a photograph of a woman's body being sliced to pieces by a large scissors, with the tag line "Made in South America . . . where life is cheap." A few days later, I happened to be invited to a Lower East Side social gathering of avowedly antisexist men; some of them identified as "effeminists," a tiny, militantly antisexist faction within the early-70s gay-liberation movement. When I described to this meeting what was happening around town with the movie *Snuff* and urged that we take some action together to protest it, I was stunned to hear these men—whose published work I once admired—sputter and spout their rationale for *not* taking action: Men should not do anything except child care if *women* decide to picket, I was told. Men should never take any action on their own on an issue of sexuality, I was chided; men have no business doing that. I felt condescended to; worse, their political arguments for inertia were utter nonsense to me, so I left the meeting in dismay. But I was determined, somehow, to find men to work with who could see their way to mobilizing some sort of meaningful protest.

Nightly, hundreds of people—mostly women, some men—

began picketing and demonstrating outside the National movie theater, where *Snuff* was playing. I assembled a bunch of men and we mounted a picket line and demonstration at the high-rise apartment building where the theater had a booking office. A smaller group of us planned to sit in at the office itself, but at the last minute we abandoned that tactic in favor of another: One Sunday morning we went to the suburban community in New Jersey where the distributor, a 60s lefty-turned-porn-entrepreneur, lived. Stepping briskly over dew-drenched lawns, we brazenly leafleted four hundred homes with his name and picture on a flyer headlined "Know Your Neighbor," with pithy quotes from press clips in which he cynically defended the sadistic and woman-hating movie from which he was profiting.

In August 1983 I was asked to help lead a workshop on pornography at a regional antisexist-men's conference at Hampshire College. Somehow a phrase from the WAP slide show flashed back to me—"Imagine men in these poses"—and I was inspired to bring along some magazines: a *Penthouse,* a *Playboy,* a *Hustler,* and several others. Something of my background in experimental theater must have come into play too, because I had an idea to conduct a theater-games–type exercise during which I would select several men at random out of the group, give each a magazine, and tell them to "do the pose" in a designated photograph. While these men were struggling into their assigned poses, I would invite the rest of the workshop participants to go from pose to pose. And I would urge the workshop participants to compare each pose to the picture it was based on and to call out comments about how to get the body position and facial expression more accurate. (Perhaps I was also remembering an indelible childhood visit to a state fair sideshow, where spectators thronged into a tent and were ushered from freak to freak.) After this carneylike stroll through a gallery of staged poses, I would reassemble the group in a circle to talk. I had no idea what would happen, or whether my crackpot workshop idea would "work." I just took a chance and tried it.

When the time came for the workshop, nearly seventy-five people arrived, women and men, mostly young, squeezed shoulder to shoulder in chairs around the room. I had not expected the place to be so full, and I began conducting the pose exercise with some trepidation.

At first there was much surprised and nervous laughter. The spectators called out comments rather eagerly, as if in fun. And the posers tried gamely to imitate the body position and facial expression in their assigned photograph. But with each successive pose, the group seemed to become more serious. It was as if the temperature of the room suddenly plunged, from high frivolity to deep solemnity. After only about a half dozen poses, I realized they had had quite enough and were about to numb out (if they had not already), so I stopped the exercise abruptly and asked everyone to sit in a circle so we could talk.

With only limited time left and palpable heaviness in the room, I realized I had to act fast so that as many people as possible could give voice to some of the roiling emotions stirred up by the experience everyone just had. I called on people as they flailed their hands, and without much prompting, they began to speak, out of diverse and intense personal reactions.

A few people spoke in emotionally remote, conceptual, and opinionated terms, delivering mini-orations about the First

Amendment, censorship, "the difference between pornography and erotica," and so forth. But these people were in the minority. Most had something else—something more pressing and personal —on their minds. Most people groped for words for how they *felt,* for words to say how they felt *doing the poses,* to explain how they felt *watching men do those poses.* They wanted to express what this experience had *meant* to them. And what came out of people's mouths blew me away. They were saying things, from their own experience, that I had never heard said. And it seemed to me that something quite unusual had happened: Something had interrupted normal thought processes and triggered new ones. Something had prompted people to *see* that which before they had only *looked at.*

Back home in New York, I began calling some men I knew, some of whom I had earlier invited to the Women Against Pornography slide show. These were men who were interested in working together against pornography in some way (most had been involved in antipornography activism to some extent). We named ourselves Men Against Pornography, and we set out as a team to conduct workshops—based on the "pose" exercise and guided discussion afterward—for various kinds of groups of men. The Pose Workshop, we called it for short.

Over the course of many meetings, we founding members of Men Against Pornography talked about some deeply felt common aspirations. Ironically, one thing we had in common was that we were not keen on belonging to a men's group, per se. What we wanted instead was a form for antisexist activism that was more than a one-shot demo—something we could sustain over a long time. And we set some specific goals for ourselves. We wanted to encourage men . . .

- to *recognize* the reality of the women who are pictured in pornography.
- to *experience* what is happening—to get past argumentative and intellectual defenses about pornography.
- to *examine* the relationship of pornography use to men's personal sexual histories.
- to *understand*—for themselves—that pornography exploits women's sexuality and manipulates men's.
- to *create change*—to take action to create meaningful consciousness, in public and in private, that pornography stands in the way of gender justice.

As it turned out, all these aspirations translated into a simple and practical method to help men *perceive:* to help men see with "new eyes."

When men "do the pose" in a picture from a pornography magazine, the effect is often a jolt of recognition: Men notice that what is happening to a woman in pornography is happening to a real person—"someone with real feelings like myself." The Pose Workshop is very forthright: no long-winded theory, no complicated jargon, no claptrap. The Pose Workshop works first at a gut level—at a language-and-concept level only later.

Although The Pose Workshop is intended as a sort of "empathy training" for men, it may be offered for either men-only groups or mixed groups of women and men. In mixed groups, both women and men participate as spectators—but only men "do the pose."

The workshop is experiential: It is designed to tap into actual sensation, actual memory, actual emotional/physical reality, and actual perception. The workshop is participatory: It is designed to set up effective circumstances in which each participant can come to new experiences, new ways of seeing, new ways of understanding. It is designed to maximize learning through participants' recognition of the meaning of their own experience. It eschews learning by being *told* or by being *criticized.*

I and other cofounders of Men Against Pornography were inspired by the radical-feminist insight that pornography is "the graphic, sexually explicit subordination of women." So it is probably no coincidence that The Pose Workshop often communicates viscerally to men the root meaning of "subordination"—as a *transaction,* as something that *happens* to someone because someone else *does* it—in a way that is concrete (literally, in "body language").

Though I have written philosophically and spoken out polemically on the subject of pornography, I am convinced of the simultaneous need for nonideological discourse among men about our perceptual relationship to pornography. To that end, The Pose Workshop prevents head trips, or intellectual defenses, that get in the way of personal understanding and real change. Specific techniques are used to avert abstract discussion or debate about, for instance, the definition of pornography or the difference between pornography and erotica. During the workshop, in fact, the word "pornography" is never even spoken by facilitators, because the word itself is such a potent cue to men's perceptions. Instead, the workshop is designed to avoid guilt trips—to be a nonjudgmental, safe space in which participants can reflect, express, and listen.

The Pose Workshop supports personal change that is "self-interested" in that it is in the interests of a participant's own best self: The workshop affirms the best potential in participants to perceive the reality of what is happening to other selves. It encourages men to take responsibility for their perceptions by helping them realize their capacity to do so.

The exercise touches nerves and gets past defenses in part because it takes some controlled risks. Even though posers are expressly told not to imitate nudity in the photographs, the experience of "doing the pose" in front of other workshop participants always raises issues of consent, power, and vulnerability. Therefore workshop facilitators bear a heavy responsibility for making certain that participants come through the experience OK.

❖

Whenever I conducted The Pose Workshop, I was meticulous about publicity. I knew that whatever was announced in advance would set up expectations that could enhance or undermine the workshop event itself. Much of men's perceptual relationship to pornography is individual, personal, and idiosyncratic. But much of men's perceptual relationship to pornography is also peer pressured and culturally prompted—a social event, shared among men, according to standards and expectations meted out by other men. Any inquiry into the subject therefore necessarily runs afoul of a pervasive pre-existing condition: Men tend to look at pornography as if other men are looking too, and men tend to see what they think other men *expect* them to see.

When I gave The Pose Workshop on a campus or as part of a conference where there was a social network or community of some sort, I very carefully specified the workshop title and exact wording of the promotional blurb so as to begin challenging male-male social pressure from the outset.

For instance, I usually specified that the workshop would be "Open to women and men." Occasionally I followed a workshop sponsor's preference and made it "Men only, please," but the more workshops I did, the more leery I became of discourse among men in all-male groups—especially about pornography—where gender-exclusivity is declared at the door. Once women are politically shut out of the discussion, that effectively tells each man to utter only that which other men will not be upset or angry to hear him say, and each man therefore stays stuck in the very genderizing peer pressures that have shaped his own perceptions of pornography.

For a man alone to look at pornography is one thing (although he is never really "alone"; he is always sharing the experience vicariously with a massive consumer class of other men).

For men together to look at men's looking is another matter entirely. It is a brand-new challenge: perceiving the act of perception.

For men to know that women are also looking at men's looking adds yet another dimension to men's moment of perceptual recognition. Without that dimension, without a social context attuned to gender politics, the men's moment of recognition is less likely to occur.

Whether men-only or mixed, the workshop was always billed as "an experiential workshop for men." This "truth in packaging" alerted women that the workshop was designed primarily as a participatory experience for men; women were welcome, but women's participation might at times be observational. Everyone had a right to know this much going in.

In my years of conducting The Pose Workshop, I never resolved an obvious imbalance in its design: The experience was designed for men, to encourage expression and exploration of their own perceptual relationship to pornography; yet without women's active presence and participation, the workshop would be less meaningful for men. The converse was not also true, however. The experience was not designed for women; in some sense men's active presence and participation were a social deterrent to women's expression and exploration of their own perceptual relationship to pornography. And I acknowledge that was a flaw in the workshop conception.

In some circumstances, an age limit needed to be specified—by stating, for instance, "Open to women and men age 18 and up"—because The Pose Workshop used materials that could not legally be sold to minors. In a college or university setting, the likely participants would presumably be old enough. But in more open-to-the-public venues, a minimum age limit was always prudent. State and municipal obscenity laws are notoriously useless against the actual harm to humans from the traffic in pornography. Such statutes are impotent to impede the pornography industry's role as sex educator of youth, for instance. Nevertheless, it would be foolhardy to invite an obscenity prosecution against

The Pose Workshop. Now and then—in the absence of an announced age limit—a parent brought a child into the workshop, so I took the parent aside beforehand to explain the sort of pictorials that would be used and to recommend that the parent reconsider the child's participation. This private communication was always persuasive.

The stated title of the workshop was tailored to the circumstance. I frequently used "What Makes Pornography 'Sexy'?: An Experiential Workshop for Men." Other possibilities included "Pornography Workshop for Changing Men" and "How to Look at Pornography: An Experiential Workshop for Men." To preserve the element of surprise, publicity never disclosed that workshop participants would be doing poses; the word "experiential" said enough.

If there was going to be a promotional paragraph in addition to the title, I always supplied the workshop sponsor with a specific and intentional text:

WHAT MAKES PORNOGRAPHY "SEXY"?: AN EXPERIENTIAL WORKSHOP FOR MEN

How are the pictures in *Penthouse, Playboy, Hustler,* etc. meant to be arousing to men—and what are those pictures actually about? Can men learn to perceive those pictures differently? Can we learn to look at those pictures so that we see what's really in them? How might that affect our view of ourselves and of women? Through a guided, experiential exercise and group discussion, this provocative workshop will explore some possible answers to these questions.

If the workshop was to be publicized through local media, I recommended a press release like the following. I wanted everything a participant learned about the workshop—from the first word to the last—to make a coherent impression, one that would eventually open "new eyes":

WORKSHOP FOR MEN TO EXPLORE
WHAT MAKES PORNOGRAPHY "SEXY"

What makes pornography "sexy" to men? How and why are men aroused by the pictures in *Penthouse, Playboy, Hustler,* etc.—and what are those pictures actually about? How does pornography function in men's lives? Can men look at those pictures so that they can see what's really in them? How could that affect men's view of themselves and of women?

[Sponsoring group name] tries to answer those questions through a workshop that creates a unique experience in which men can begin to deal honestly and openly with their perceptions of pornography.

[Sponsoring group name] will conduct this provocative workshop [date, time, place]. Enrollment is limited to 40 women and men age 18 and older. For reservations or more information, call [telephone number].

In choosing a room for the workshop, I preferred the space to be big and comfortable, like a lounge, with carpeting and movable furniture—cushioned sofas, chairs, and various kinds of objects. There needed to be doors that closed once the workshop began and no passerby traffic, so people who were not participants would not walk through accidentally. I shunned classrooms with bolted-down desks. And if a group of more than forty people was expected, I requested a stage or raised platform upon which posers could be seen by everyone in the room. Often presenters asked me, "Well, how do you want the room set up?" and I'd say, "Whatever it is—just leave it." I wanted people upon arrival to sit anywhere, uneventfully, without any cues from the room about what was going to happen next.

❖

Over the years, news about The Pose Workshop was effectively spread by many diverse media—TV, newspapers, magazines, word-of-mouth. The design of The Pose Workshop was so simple, it was readily paraphrasable in twenty-five words or less ("They have men do poses from pornography magazines—whoa!—and everyone calls out comments to get the men to pose more like the picture!"). This basic format could be retold and passed along in a variety of ways, no matter how colloquial. And almost always, some version of the workshop's message got passed along as well ("When men look at men posing like pictures in pornography, the men begin to see the women as real people—like themselves"). The meaning of The Pose Workshop got through even to people who never experienced it; The Pose Workshop "worked" when people simply heard about it. Thus the action of facilitating a Pose Workshop—whether news of the event was broadcast or simply whispered down the lane—had a remarkable power to make multiple impressions, in the lives of countless people.

I once attended a conference about sexual harassment where a young man stood up and started telling people about The Pose

Workshop, which had been described to him by his teacher in a women's studies class. And this young man went on and on about the workshop—what a signal event it was in his reflection on his own personal sexual values—even though he had never even experienced it; he had only heard about it from his teacher. Afterward I introduced myself to him and asked what women's studies class he took. When he told me, I remembered it: "I did The Pose Workshop for that teacher five years ago," I told him. I also recalled—though I did not say—that this particular women's studies teacher was certifiably hostile to feminist antipornography efforts. Yet five years later she was still talking about The Pose Workshop in class, and amazingly this young male student got its import from her hearsay anyway.

I took great care in the management of media access. I never allowed cameras of any kind into the workshop, although I was often asked to. Occasionally I let a TV news crew interview someone talking about the experience afterward. But I felt strongly that photographing The Pose Workshop experience would be a serious violation of participants' privacy rights, one that nobody could knowledgeably consent to in advance.

Occasionally I let print journalists in, but only to be participant-observers, and news and feature stories were written about The Pose Workshop from inside on that basis. But I felt obliged to be very controlling about workshop confidentiality, and I always told journalists beforehand, "Don't use any identifying details about anyone."

Soon after Men Against Pornography began offering The Pose Workshop, *Ms.* magazine ran a story about it and we were contacted by producers of several television talk shows to present and discuss it on the air. We developed a TV version, which I conducted in several regional TV markets and on two national talk shows as well, *Sally Jessy Raphael* and *Donahue* (the latter was syndicated around the world). For television I supplied three pictorial spreads pasted onto posterboard with black rectangles placed over each model's breasts, vagina, and/or anus. These suitable-for-TV photographs could then be scanned and transmitted to monitors visible to men in the studio as they "did" each pose. Simultaneously, each modified photo appeared on home viewers' screens as an insert within the video frame that showed the man "doing" that particular pose. In television terms, this split-screen image made the point of The Pose Workshop with startling graphic impact. Before each show was taped, I preselected men from the studio audience who would agree to "do a pose" on air. In a regular workshop, they would have been picked at random and not told what they would be asked to do. But because this exposure was going to be public, I always went out in front of the studio audience during the warm-up period, explained exactly what was going to be done (naturally, this elicited laughs, both expectant and nervous), and asked for two or three men to volunteer to pose on camera. Despite these slight changes in the workshop format to accommodate broadcast standards, posers' responses were remarkably in sync with the personal observations men typically made in the small-group version.

For more than a decade I committed to promoting The Pose Workshop through a variety of communications media, because seeing it, reading about it, retelling it, or even just hearing about it had such a far-reaching and memorable effect on individual sexual relationships to pornography. One time, someone with an academic background in social science did a follow-up study with individuals who six months earlier had gone through a Pose Workshop I conducted. The extraordinary result of this research was the finding that most of the individuals talked about the workshop experience as if it had just happened, still fresh in their minds. The researcher told me that people rarely remember *anything* that vividly.

Winning hearts and minds on the issue of pornography means, for many men, prompting change at some very deep personal and sexual levels. For some, The Pose Workshop experience helped shake loose a stuck perception pattern so that it could be held up to view for a change.

❖

Choosing which magazines and photos to use was the first crucial step in preparation. Whenever I cofacilitated a Pose Workshop with other men, we were all involved in making the selection. This was an unusual experience in itself: men looking at pictures that would be used by men posing in a workshop about how men look at pornography, and how men look at men's looking.

The objective was to select a picture from each of at least six different magazines, to be the visual reference for each of six poses during a workshop. The magazines were kept intact; the photos were not torn out. This photo-selection process—whether done alone or with a team of cofacilitators—always felt to me like a grim obligation. I recall going somewhat numb and tense deliberating over which pictures to use.

Over time, through trial and error, these became the criteria that we found produced the best workshop results:

The six magazines worked best if they represented a range of titles—some of which could be expected to be familiar to men in the workshop and some of which might not. I always included one or two recent issues of *Playboy* and *Penthouse* on the not-rash presumption that they would generally be recognized. Then I added one to four titles less mainstream but generally available at newsstands, kiosks, and convenience stores, such as *Genesis, Stag, Adam,* or *Cheri*. Depending on the circumstances I sometimes included a title that could evidently be purchased only at an "adult" or "XXX" store. I found that The Pose Workshop was eminently effective with ordinary men's magazines such as *Playboy* and *Penthouse,* but less-mainstream titles added a dimension, especially as participants recognized for themselves the similarities among them all. Occasionally men voiced their own recognition that the poses—stripped of "production values" such as lighting, sets, and props—seemed variations on the same theme: women constrained and displayed, not inhabiting their own bodies with anything resembling physical integrity or congruity.

We also found that the most useful pictures showed a whole body, photographed alone. Pictures showing only part of a torso would not give enough information to the poser. Moreover, a picture with more than one woman in it could not be imitated by a solitary poser. This limited The Pose Workshop's scope, of course, since contrived "lesbian" poses are de rigueur in "men's sophisticates." The Pose Workshop concept—men watching other men in poses from pornography—was already close enough to the limit of public homoeroticism that most male participants could comfortably withstand. Asking two men to duplicate a duo pose from pornography would probably introduce a distraction from which the workshop might never recover, because what was happening between the two posers would command more attention than what was happening between the poser and the spectators.

The most effective pictures also showed the body in a pose of some complexity—not "just standing there" or "just lying there, looking at the camera." Typically hips or buttocks were thrown up or out, a back was arched or torqued, a neck was bent, the body seemed not so much inhabited as exhibited. Such poses could be readily replicated by someone lying or kneeling on the floor or a sofa, with or without props or furnishings, or leaning against something.

Very early on, the cofounding members of Men Against Pornography learned that no picture should be used in a live workshop without having been "pretested" among ourselves. At the beginning we held meetings to "do the poses" in all the photographs we chose. That way we formed a personal sense memory of what it feels like, from the inside, to "do" each pose on the workshop agenda. But more important, we learned to recognize which pictured poses might seem easy at first glance but turn out to be quite dangerous—because, perhaps, they stressed or sent muscles into spasm. Without personally "pretesting" each pose, a facilitator could never know this. Several of the poses I've used in workshops have been extremely painful to hold for more than a few seconds. They required a level of flexibility and muscle tone that even gymnastically fit men in their early twenties do not often have. A few poses I have used could cause serious distress if held for very long. We in MAP stopped using a particular bondage magazine, moreover, because it was simply too emotionally wrenching to do *any* of the poses in it. From my experience pretesting poses among colleagues in MAP, I formed my own sense of what the level of physical or emotional difficulty in a photo is—so that as a facilitator I could know in advance which pose I should not give to anyone with evident back problems, for instance, and so that the workshop did not inadvertently precipitate a physical or psychological emergency.

Early MAP meetings were a precursor to the discussions that in real workshops always followed the posing exercise. We practiced "doing" the pose in the pictures to be used. We talked back and forth informally about how it felt and about the mechanics of what was going on; we gave each other comments to help get the pose more accurate.

During tryouts of The Pose Workshop concept at those early MAP meetings, I first discovered for myself a strange phenomenon: Whenever I was "doing a pose" I experienced a distinct discrepancy between the body position I was in and the facial expression that I had to "put on" in order to imitate the pose "convincingly." My face felt discordant with the physical experience of the rest of me. I would look at a photograph, get into the pose, turn and twist my body according to how I was coached by my fellow MAPers—but when I consulted the photograph again in order to match the facial expression just right, I found that the face I now had to "put on" had no coherent relationship to the sensations in my body below the neck. I found this out only when "inside" the pose, really doing it: I recall the feeling vividly, as though my head and face were detached from my body, as if I were severed at the neck. For me and the cofacilitators of The Pose Workshop, this recognition was one of the first personal tip-offs about the inauthenticity of affect, the internal dislocation of emotion, and the lack of bodily integrity that occur in the body of the woman who is posing before the camera. For Pose Workshop facilitators, this was thus "extracurricular" empathy training. I remembered from such rehearsals how this alienating experience feels and looks, so that whenever I noticed a poser experience a similar internal alienation or dissociation, I could recognize the experience; it was personally familiar.

Just *looking* at such a photograph—before pretesting any poses—I might never have observed or detected this "alienation effect." Over the years I witnessed many men obviously unnerved by the experience—in part, I suspect, because most men are not in the habit of enforcing, inside themselves, such extreme emotional and physical dislocations during sex. For most men, what their body is feeling shows up spontaneously in their expression, unmediated by the self-objectifying question "How does my face look now?" Thus for many men, including myself, "doing the pose" was a startlingly visceral introduction to the "self-splitting" that female models perform in order to qualify as "sexy" in a camera's lens. From the perspective of the camera—and hence male consumers' eyes—the face and body of the woman appear as a visual unity. But in the emotional and physical sensations of an actual human being "doing the pose," face and body feel split asunder. Once having experienced this split myself, I could better recognize when a poser was discovering the "alienation effect" kinesthetically for himself but unable to talk about it, and I could better help him name the experience for himself.

Once I picked up on this "alienation effect" rehearsing The Pose Workshop, I began to be able to detect it in photographs even before pretesting the pictured pose. And as I became more observant about that phenomenon, I recognized it as the stock in trade of "men's sophisticate" photography: the face not spontaneous, the spinal column curved solely for vaginal or rectal display, the model's facial affect quite literally out of touch with her body, intimations of dislocation or restraint, deference to a voyeur's viewpoint. Such photos were not hard to find; they were in virtually every magazine.

Among MAP's preparations for The Pose Workshop was also an unusual vocabulary exercise: We practiced talking about pictures using only words that are descriptive, concrete, and emotionally neutral. Before conducting a live workshop, we would literally sit around looking at an assortment of photographs one by one, and we would practice describing the pictures out loud to one another without using subjective, interpretive, or culturally loaded language such as "desire" or "sexy" or "Oh, she looks like she really wants it" or "She's really hot" or "She's thinking, 'Give it to me, big guy.'" Instead, we studiously practiced making concrete, direct, and objective observations: "She's looking off into the middle distance," "She's staring vacantly; her eyes are not focusing on anything in particular," "Her lips are moist and slightly parted," "Her face is limp," "Her knees are spread," "Her back is swayed," "Her buttocks are raised above her shoulders," and so forth. This vocabulary exercise was not as easy as it sounds. Emotive and sexually suggestive language tended to come more readily to mind. But with practice and concentration, we facilitators-in-training became more adept at speaking a descriptive language about the photographs that was removed from the "button-pushing" language customarily associated with "sexy" pictures.

Early on, I found that in The Pose Workshop context the word "pornography" tended to get in the way of perception; it tended to frame what a male viewer saw according to what he *expected* to see, and the very word often prompted mental digressions that prevented both his naming of his own experience and his recognition of anyone else's. So I urged my fellow facilitators never to speak the word "pornography" during The Pose Workshop: If the word "pornography" was to appear at all, it should be only in publicity—never on the lips of a pose-exercise conductor or a discussion leader. Workshop participants were free to use whatever words they wanted, of course; but to be most effective, facilitators had to be circumspect in their vocabulary. Sitting around together, prepping to conduct a workshop, became an excellent opportunity to practice not using the word "pornography." Thus we practiced describing each picture very particularly, thinking, "What exactly am I looking at?" then saying so, as objectively as possible. Since the overall goal of the workshop was to help participants perceive the reality of someone else (even though a camera had looked at that person first), this vocabulary exercise helped us develop an important facilitation skill.

It was my consistent experience that once a facilitator or discussion leader inadvertently uttered the word "pornography," a coded signal seemed to have been sent, giving participants permission—indeed, urging them—to evade their own process of perceptual discovery. If by chance a facilitator *did* lend a value-laden name to any picture while The Pose Workshop was in progress—especially if a facilitator slipped and spoke the word "pornography"—the discussion would inevitably veer off into any of several abstract and circuit-jamming detours. But during a Pose Workshop the word "pornography" was functionally unnecessary, because the facilitator's words did not *have* to carry an opinion, speculate on a definition, or imply a valuation; for all practical purposes the facilitator needed do no more than refer participants' attention to the actual pictures and magazines that had already been shown in the room. So I learned to keep in mind several neutral "pointing" words for situational use during any workshop I conducted: "these pictures," "pictures like these," "pictures in magazines," "magazines like the ones you just saw," and so forth. My use of such referential language contributed to a discussion climate that participants often commented on favorably because it seemed to them "nonjudgmental." But its real purpose lay much deeper: to encourage participants to home in on their own powers of perception.

Practicing talking this way helped me and other workshop leaders to model appropriate coaching comments from spectators. Sometimes while holding up the photo that the poser was trying to match, I would notice something in the picture that spectators had not yet commented on, so I would say something to the poser like "Look off into the distance and don't focus on anything." I often chimed in with coaching about the poser's face because, I noted, spectators initially paid most attention below the model's neck. I would often tell the poser, "Let your face go limp"— because by then he was in such contortions that he was grimacing or gritting his teeth and he could not possibly approximate the photo until—rather awkwardly—he had let go of control over his ocular and facial muscles. Conducting The Pose Workshop was a weird and unnatural thing to do, I have to admit. I usually got through it by going "on automatic." So especially during the pose-and-coach period, it was important for me to know I had available a practiced vocabulary that I could rely on to neutralize distracting emotional inflection.

Vocabulary practice with cofacilitators beforehand also came in handy for leading group discussions, because it helped me to tune in and respond instantaneously when participants talked about the photos in language loaded with emotive projections and inference. A participant might say something like "Oh, she looks like she really wants it," at which point I might prompt very straightforwardly, "What exactly did you see in the picture that suggested that to you?" Neither I nor other discussion leaders ever told participants what to think, believe, or feel; but we frequently focused participants' attention—to help them learn a way of not only *looking* at the photo but of really *seeing* it—and the best way to do that was with direct questions or neutrally descriptive restatements that drew out and led participants to concrete observations. During the course of a Pose Workshop, it was almost as though each photograph became an evidentiary document to be parsed by an ad-hoc committee, one voice and viewer at a time. To help participants get past conventional "wisdom" about models' motive, desire, and intent—all those received and restimulated attributions of "sexiness" that come from having been sucked and suckered into an industry that sells sex as a commodity—our only tools at hand were words. And the best ones, I found, were unadorned.

Six poses was about the maximum that any group could

withstand. Four or five worked fine. But after six, the dramatic arc of the exercise turned from enjoyment to angry estrangement very fast. Assuming poses from newsstand magazines like *Penthouse* and *Playboy* with a few less-mainstream publications thrown in, the workshop generally started out at a level of jollity and self-conscious good humor. With each successive pose, however, the group mood became more tense, chilly, and creepy as people caught on to what was happening and realized what they were doing.

Though I tried to keep in mind who was given which picture and where they went in the room, I could never remember accurately. Nevertheless I always memorized the sequence in which the pictures would be given out, so that during the pose exercise, the poses would be conducted in my preplanned order.

I sometimes planned a sequence of photos from which participants could infer that there was not much difference between what was happening in the photo from *Penthouse,* for instance, and what was happening in a triple-X bondage magazine. Such sequencing was easy to achieve, and it sometimes subtly modified people's perspective about "where you draw the line." *Oh, here's just an ordinary beaver shot,* a participant might think. *But it's not really so different from over there where she's tied up on a plank with a ball gag in her mouth. It's the same inauthenticity. Her body is just as constrained by someone else's imagination.*

I always began The Pose Workshop suddenly, by surprise. I would walk into the room where the participants had already assembled;

with no introduction I would say, "Hi, I'm John Stoltenberg"; then without further ado I'd announce, "Now, I'd like to start the workshop by counting off all the men in the room by [a certain number]. You'll understand why later. Be sure to remember your number. One, two, three . . ." No hemming-and-hawing, no shilly-shallying—and suddenly all the men were counting off a number out loud.

However perplexed men may have been to be singled out this way, they generally went along, even announcing their own number with gusto. This simple preliminary task—with its subtle hint of gender-bonding and peer pressure—had an uncanny effect. It abruptly started the process by which posers were selected randomly; and it became a remarkably reliable technique for getting The Pose Workshop off the ground, because it got the men concentrating on doing something I had asked them to do—even before they knew what they were doing or why.

Before I walked into that room, though, I had to calculate what number to have the men count off by. I eyeballed the crowd, counted how many men were present, then did simple math in my head: [Number of men in the room] divided by [number of poses I would be using] equals [number to count off by]. Suppose, for instance, twenty-four men had arrived and I wanted to select six of them to be posers—I would have all the men count off by four. This mental exercise became for me an agreeable distraction, and I have no doubt it helped me cope with the rather disagreeable things I was about to do next.

Once all the men had counted off, I chose one of the count-off numbers and said, "OK, now I'd like to ask all the 2s [for instance] to gather in the center of the room. The rest of you, please wait a minute." Whether self-consciously or with bravado, the men whose number was "2" then ambled wherever I asked them to. They still did not have a clue as to what was going on; meanwhile everyone else in the workshop was already watching them. Then and only then did I reveal my pile of magazines, which I had kept under wraps in an opaque plastic bag. And before anyone had a moment to register what was happening, I said to the group of six, "Now I'm going to give each of you a picture from a magazine." I always used the phrase "Now I'm going to . . . "—even as I was *doing* it—and very briskly, I gave a magazine to each randomly selected man. I'd hand him the whole publication already turned open to the page where the preselected photo appeared (so the magazine title was not yet visible), and I would say to each in turn, "This is your picture . . . this is your picture . . . ," and so forth. By the time I distributed the pictures, I said very directly, as if offering the most ordinary information in the world, "And I'm going to ask each of you to do the pose in that picture."

That was always a dramatic high point, and inevitably there were audible responses from the audience—plus a range of reactions from the men who until now had been standing there unawares, simply holding onto their assigned picture as if it was something secure to cling to. I ignored the reaction, or acknowledged it but briefly, and went right on. "Try to imitate everything about the pose except the nudity—."

Another reaction now usually swept the room—from gasps to guffaws, giggles to groans. "Find a place somewhere around the room and use whatever furniture or props you need to get the pose accurate. Take a few minutes and try to get the pose as accurate as you can."

I continued talking, in a calm, steady, reassuring voice, repeating and elaborating on the instruction: "Take your time. You can do your pose anywhere in this room. Use whatever furniture or props you need. Everybody else, just relax for a few minutes. Get as close as you can to the pose and the face—and then relax. Just put the magazine down on the floor, face-up so the picture is visible, and just relax where you are. Find the pose by yourself. Find a place to do the pose—the furniture, the cushions, whatever you need. And then once you have done it, put the magazine down and relax wherever you are."

I allowed a couple minutes for all the men with magazines to take in the geography and get their bearings, choose a location in the room, move around furniture as necessary, and get into their assigned pose. Meanwhile I kept everybody else waiting expectantly. Although typically a group started out chuckling nervously, especially when the photographs were being distributed, the task at hand—doing the pose—soon became everyone's focus.

As nominal leader of these odd proceedings, I deemed my assurance, directness, and timing to be most important during the first critical moments. A deliberate element of surprise kept matters moving lightheartedly past points that might have bogged down if participants had time to reflect. To keep the pace from foundering at the start, I made certain that my batch of magazines was prepared for quick distribution. Sometime prior to the workshop, the afternoon or evening before, I folded the magazines one inside another, so that each would automatically fall open to the picture I intended to give a poser. I preselected the sequence of pictures at the same time, folding the last around the outside and collapsing the first into the inside. Before I closed the bundle, I put a bookmark into the centermost, which I would open and hand out first. Such exacting attention to the mechanics of magazine assembly—including a few practice efforts at brisk distribution—prevented awkward spills or delays that could derail momentum during a live workshop.

To workshop participants, my count-off method of selecting posers seemed apparently random, but there were times when I needed to influence "chance." If in counting off the men I noticed someone whose physical condition or disability would have made his doing any pose obviously difficult, I made a mental note of whatever number he got—and I simply remembered not to call on men with that number. In a room of thirty men who were counting off by five, for instance, I might notice there was a 3 who was going to have a serious physical problem getting into any pose. Without calling special attention to his condition, I simply announced at the appropriate time, "All the 4s come into the center of the room," "All the 1s," or "All the 5s." Any number but 3. To do this I had to concentrate and think fast—like a poker player keeping track of all the cards in the deck.

I discovered another discreet way to select out a poser who may be at risk, and it required that I have a sense memory of the physical difficulty of every pose I had selected and pretested. Say that I had gathered all the 4s in the center of the room, and say I suddenly noticed that one had an evident physical limitation—he was stiff or quite out of shape. I made certain to give this individual a photograph that I already knew was not as physically challenging as the rest of the pictures in my pile. Doing that particular pose may have had similar subjective effects, but it was unlikely, I knew from prior testing, to send his back into spasm. I remember one innocuous but dangerous pose—I used it a lot but I was always careful never to give it to someone who was not evidently physically fit: The woman wears stiletto heels and stands bent over at the waist, her rectum to the camera, and she apparently leans over onto a support of some sort, so that her head and shoulders are lower than her buttocks. To the casual viewer, this pose did not look particularly difficult, but I have watched in alarm as many a young man, lean and limber, began throbbing uncontrollably in the muscles of his legs, seized by tension in his back, after but seconds doing this pose. He might well have grinned and borne the experience without damage. But for anyone not so athletic, a picture of a woman posed languidly on a chaise longue was always a better choice.

At some point I knew that someone directed to pose would say, "No. I don't want to. I don't want to do this." It had to happen sometime, and I knew in advance there would be only one ethically appropriate response: "Thank you very much." And then: "Is there someone else?" (If no replacement volunteered for the exercise, I would simply eliminate a pose; if I was planning six, I'd do five.)

Only once in my experience have any male participants flat-out refused. I was conducting The Pose Workshop for a group of students at a vocational high school in New York City, in a rather chilly classroom with desks bolted down, and two of the young men—who swaggered into the workshop in the midst of far more peer pressure than this exercise could ever generate—just said no. I believed it morally imperative that if anyone during The Pose

Workshop ever said no at any point, that was it; they didn't do it. No questions asked. Theoretically, of course, *everyone* in the room could say no. But that never happened to me.

In truth, The Pose Workshop always crossed a line of consent. It asked people to agree to do something—imitate the pose in a picture—before they could possibly know the full physical or emotional meaning of what it was that they were being asked to do. What made it all worthwhile (or so I justified The Pose Workshop in my own mind) was that they could not *find out* that meaning otherwise. But for me as a leader, this was always the hardest and morally most dubious part of conducting The Pose Workshop: asking people to do something that they could not possibly consent to knowledgeably, but asking them anyway, because what they were about to learn experientially would be edifying in ways that other means of communication simply could not be. Inch-by-inch, individuals' lines of consent got crossed, even as their spirits were borne along by amusement and group appreciation. A man had already counted off, had already accepted a photograph as "his," had already shuffled off to do his pose in a corner—just as other men seemed to be doing elsewhere in the room without visible or audible complaint, so how bad could this be?—and before he knew what was happening, he was struggling into a compromising position in front of dozens of other people who may have been close friends or complete strangers, and before he knew it, he was following their orders, adjusting his body and affect according to their coaching and commands, making a spectacle of himself, apparently at the whim of a crowd. The Pose Workshop not only *simulated* erosion of personal choice-making; the workshop *reenacted* it, restimulating deep human fears of abandonment, loss of self-possession, humiliation, vulnerability, exposure, helplessness—albeit in as carefully monitored a social environment as possible. Gradually this structured diminishment of the capacity for integrated choice-making started hitting people—at a very deep physical and emotional level, far below the surface of everyday chatter. As a Pose Workshop leader I never gave away the secret of this impact or explained what was really happening—but like clockwork, the scenario of The Pose Workshop would steadily replicate the palpable experience of personal powerlessness that men are ordinarily entitled to stand outside of, especially as voyeur-consumers in the pornography market. This workshop process reached most participants on at least some gut level, I believe. The majority of men who went through it realized something about what they had been interpreting as "sexy" that they had no conscious idea of before.

In the "real world," of course, women's consent is rarely ever calibrated with such precision, and women commonly experience such inch-by-inch erosion of autonomy and constraint of volition without men's paying anything resembling such supersensitive attention. Interestingly, though, when men in The Pose Workshop witnessed this dynamic happening to a man—even in circumstances in which, strictly speaking, the man could always choose to stop—the experience became more visible, and the dynamic became more recognizable.

Optimally the workshop was scheduled to run for an hour and a half, and I allowed the first twenty to thirty minutes for counting off and posing. About two minutes after the count-off—after the posers had each found a place in the room and temporarily done their pose, put down their magazine, and relaxed—I went to the first magazine picture I had handed out, now lying on the floor somewhere in the room, and I ascertained whose pose it was. I asked that particular poser to stay where he was and I took the magazine in hand; meanwhile I directed everyone else, including all the other posers, to stand together as an audience. I asked the other posers to leave their own magazine behind on the floor, or wherever it was, and join this gathering gallery of spectators too. And I guided everyone into a cluster so that they could observe the poser from approximately the same angle of vision. I held up the picture from the first poser's magazine so that everyone could see it, and I said, "Now, while this man is doing the pose in this picture, I'm going to ask you all to call out instructions to him to help him get the pose as accurate as possible. Be specific. Tell him exactly what he should do with his face and body to get the pose as accurate as possible. Coach him. Help him out." I made sure everyone in the spectator crowd had a chance to see the picture up close; I made sure everyone could look back and forth a few times to compare the man posing to the picture he was trying to approximate. I also gave the poser one last chance to look at the picture—but from then on he became dependent on the group's comments for guidance. If the group was large, I made sure everyone could see the poser as clearly as possible, and I did the best I could to hold the picture close to spectators' eyes and at the same time stay out of their sight line to the poser. "Give him comments to help him get the pose more accurate," I continued encouragingly. If someone in the crowd made a subjective joke such as, "Look like you want it, baby!" I simply offered a quick correction, saying, "Give him specific directions, specific concrete comments. Help him out, help him get the pose accurate."

I kept my eye on the poser, and I did not hesitate to give him my own direction too: "Lick your lips . . . turn your head to the left more . . . now look up . . ." From having done the poses myself—and remembering them from the "inside"—I could sometimes give specific directions that spectators did not readily think of. Such coaching by the leader also set a clear example for the spectators, so they tended to call out their own comments in a descriptive and objective voice as asked. If there were cofacilitators, they would call out coaching too.

Frequently spectators really got into it—and often women were the most vocal. I often heard women's voices join in the coaching first, louder and more insistent than men's. There would seem to be an audible pleasure in the room, because women seemed to experience the pose exercise as a turning of the tables (and many said so later, during the discussion period). Fine, I thought. Let it be. If male spectators seemed to be quieter, more reluctant to chip in with directions to the posers, perhaps sinking silently into some sober private reverie, that was fine too, I realized. Whatever group dynamics occurred during the pose exercise, whatever audible difference there may have been between men's and women's participation, I could always count on someone to make an illuminating point about it later.

Each pose lasted not much longer than a minute or two (though to the poser it may well have seemed an eternity). There was always laughter and emotional discharge of many sorts. I never "played" to it—I tried never to become the performer myself—but I also tried not to indicate that there might be anything "wrong" with any particular audience reaction. Let it be, I told myself; let participants have whatever experience they're having—because later they will talk about it, and their own reactions to others' reactions would be grist for that discourse. I knew I needed to stand guard against emotive and culturally loaded coaching ("Look like you want it" and such); that was when I had to "edit" slightly, by modeling a more objective command. But the joking, the emotional discharge, the whatever—I didn't worry about it. I came to think that there was nothing that could happen during The Pose Workshop that was bad. If the group got gloomy, fine; that could prompt useful reflection. If the group got hilariously carried away for a while, that was fine too. There was no range of emotional discharge by spectators that would not become useful later on, I assumed, because someone would remember the fresh emotional experience and spontaneously find words for it.

Despite such blithe optimism, I learned the hard way that I needed to watch out for potential problems. In my ten years' experience conducting The Pose Workshop in a wide range of circumstances, I learned to anticipate several sorts of things that could occasionally go wrong during the posing exercise. Some were not serious, but some turned out to be very serious indeed. Anyone with a notion of conducting The Pose Workshop from reading this book should be fully apprised of such risks, make photo edits accordingly, and be able to intervene promptly before any poser gets hurt. Here are the problems that sometimes happened:

- **"Mirror imaging"** was easy to fix, with no harm done. Sometimes a poser simply got his left and right reversed, a common mistake under such disconcerting circumstances. I quickly repositioned him, so that from the spectators' point of view he would *match* the picture, rather than *reflect* it.

- **"Loners"** seemed to drift away from the "spectator" group into private anger or distress. Sometimes one or two people would drop out, hang back, or stop participating after a few poses; they would shrink to the far corners of the room, declining any further to watch the poser, look at the pictures, or call out comments. Any group's collective mood could swing very suddenly from upbeat nervous laughter to a tense, tacit recognition that this pose business had an unforeseen downside. But for some individuals, there was no "up" to begin with: They *started out* at a level of acute, personal discomfort, so they experienced, additionally, estrangement and isolation from other people's levity. In due course, "loners" would have ample opportunity to vent their feelings about this conflict during the discussion period—but they did not know that yet, and they might not even have known what feelings they were having, so they simply withdrew and shut off. Given the extent of sexual assault in society, and given the great likelihood that in any grouping of people there will be survivors present, it was only realistic to surmise that The Pose Workshop experience sometimes triggered painful and unpleasant personal memories far beyond its scope or stated purpose. I confess to having found but limited means with which to take responsibility for this fact. To my chagrin I learned that no one individual could ever conduct the workshop and keep track of every personal reaction. There was way too much to concentrate on at once. My choice was to let "loners" be—not to call particular attention to them and not necessarily engage them in any way—and yet, along with any other co-facilitators in the room, always to keep an eye out, in case someone clearly needed comfort or some affirming human contact.

- **"Pandering"**: Now and then I encountered a poser who opted to distance himself from the experience by lampooning the pose, going for laughs as if to subvert the premise of the workshop exercise. When his turn came to "do the pose," he would camp it up, "play to the pit," or act like a female impersonator, perhaps audibly seeking spectators' reaction. He would caricature the woman in the pose rather than "do" the pose as asked. In my experience conducting The Pose Workshop, I almost always found such pandering to be a reliable indicator of what the poser would say during discussion. When asked later how he felt posing, he inevitably said something like, "Well, I thought it was a hoot, I loved it"; he tended to opine (more out of First Amendment fundamentalism and/or gay-lib chauvinism than any fact base), "All those women love it, you know. They get paid for it, after all"; and sometimes he even admitted, "I would really *love* to have that much admiration by horny men." Whenever I noticed a poser was "pandering," I tried to tone it down the best I could by soberly giving specific directions. I had only modest success with this tactic. So now and then, if I had a sixth sense that some-one was likely to "pander"—perhaps in exhibitionist rebellion against what he presumed were the stacked-deck "antipornography politics" of the setup—I simply, and silently, weeded him out during the count-off.

- **"Nervous spasming"** was a signal, I learned (from doing the poses myself), of potentially painful nervous or muscular tension. Even if the poser was relatively fit, this could turn into a serious problem because the poser might be used to toughing it out athletically or exercis-ing through the pain. I always checked in verbally to make sure he knew he could quit at any time. If the poser was older or not in good physical condition—someone from whom I did not get a sixth sense he would be physically OK—my most prudent option, for safety's sake, was to interrupt the pose.

- **"Emotional accidents"** could happen, and this required of me a split focus that was no mean feat: I had to be a kind of cheerleader for the spectators; meanwhile I had to block out some of my own emotional reactions in order to conduct the exercise expediently. Strictly speaking, I was overstepping an individual poser's zone of informed and knowledgeable consent, so I felt addi-tionally obliged to watch out for the emotional and physical well-being of the person doing the pose. He might not stop when he needed to. He might try to tough it out. He might exceed his own limitations—because he was on display, on the spot, because everyone was watching and urging him on. Because he had already gotten that far, he might not have the nerve to say, "I want to stop" or "I can't do this anymore." Sometimes the exercise restimulated some long-buried abuse, incest, or sexual humiliation—in the middle of doing the pose, a man's painful memory from childhood could come crashing back, without any forewarning. The poser was always in a *very* vulnerable position; I had to watch out for him so that I could interrupt the pose instantly at the slightest indication he was in trouble. If I had any doubt in my mind, I asked the poser, "Are you all right? Are you doing OK?" He of course said yes; then I made sure that I believed him. If I sensed the poser was in trouble, I simply stopped the pose: I said, "Thank you, thank you"—even if he did not come near approximating the pose. Or sometimes I made some steadying physical contact—put my hand on his shoulder or on his back—and asked, "Are you OK?" Whatever my intervention to avert an emotional accident, it had to happen very quickly, and I was always on surer ground if there was at least one other trained facilitator in the room as a spotter. Even when a particular poser was not evidently in pain or not suddenly in emotional trouble, I felt there was always a risky critical judgment call: How much longer could he take it? How close to the picture should he be expected to get? If the poser seemed to be doing OK, I would sometimes consult the crowd's judgment by asking, "Has he got it? What do you think?" Yes, some spectators might nod or say—so I would tell the poser, "Thank you," and lead the crowd in giving him a round of applause. My question might also elicit another round of coaching to fine-tune the pose, and I might end the pose after that. Sometimes I noticed the poser was in emotional or physical trouble before anyone else—even the spotter—had a clue, and I interrupted it. At such moments it was crucial that there was a spotter ready to move in, to go to the poser immediately and steady or comfort him however necessary, in order that I could move on to conduct the next pose. The decision about how long to let a pose go involved the poser's stamina and physical condition, the crowd's changing temperament, the dramatic pace of the workshop—variables that I mentally processed all at the same time. Keeping my complete attention on both the spectators and the posers became very tricky and intense, but I tried conscientiously never to let any poser go past his private pain level.

One of the reasons for The Pose Workshop's effectiveness also made it an actual—though controlled—risk: The Pose Workshop structure brought men close to the very vulnerability that pornography is made of, the very powerlessness that pornography could not be produced without, the very subordination that men normally think of as "sexy" so long as it is happening to somebody else. For exactly that reason, I believe that The Pose Workshop should never be attempted except by practiced facilitators who are themselves on empathy alert—in order to catch an emotional accident before it happens.

Whenever I ended a pose—whether to avert an emotional accident or simply because the pose had been reasonably well achieved—I said "thank you" to the poser and I said to the spectators, "Let's give him a hand." Their ready applause—as much from relief as congratulation—provided a quick moment when I double-checked that the poser had come through the experience OK. To help him reacclimate, I might offer him a hand on his shoulder or help him to his feet. As soon as the applause tapered off, I held up the magazine so that everyone could now see the cover for the first time, and I identified it straightforwardly and factually: "That was a picture from *Playboy*," "That was a picture from *Penthouse*," or whatever the magazine title. I put it down or passed it to a cofacilitator, just to get it out of the way; then I announced, "Let's go to the next." I went directly to the next magazine, picked it up, held it up to view and said, "Whose pose is this?" The man who had been handed that picture then came forward from the crowd, and I asked him to assume the pose (although by now the pattern had been established and he generally got right into it on his own). "Help him out," I coaxed the crowd again. "Be specific. Tell him concretely how he should pose his body to match the picture. Tell him specifically how to pose his face . . ." This went on as many times as there were posers. And never did I utter the word "pornography."

The pictorial material I used in The Pose Workshop was always "heterosexual"—made of women's bodies for sale to men. Pre-workshop publicity always made specific reference to *Playboy*, *Penthouse*, and such, so men who attended may have self-selected and thus been disproportionately heterosexual. Yet even when I presented the workshop in a context where most of the men could be presumed to be gay—such as during a conference on lesbian and gay rights—my choice was always to use publications picturing women for sale to men. I never conducted The Pose Workshop using pictures from gay men's magazines, or, for that matter, from magazines such as *Playgirl* or *Women on Top,* which are ostensibly edited for women but always displayed on newsstands next to magazines like *Mandate, Torso, Jock, Honcho,* and others marketed overtly to gay men.

In my experience, The Pose Workshop seemed to have a relevant effect for gay men particularly *because* the pictures were of women. For the poser or spectator who is gay, of course, The Pose Workshop pushed slightly different buttons than it did for a man who is heterosexual—in part because the poser himself might become an erotic "object" once he got into the pose. Yet I have heard many gay men report during discussions how surprised they were to realize, as a spectator, that they experienced a "homoerotic" feeling when another man replicated a pose or attitude derived from heterosexual men's pornography. Thus for some gay men, The Pose Workshop functioned as an object lesson (literally and figuratively) about the relationship between the sexual subordination of women and what most men grow up perceiving to be "sexy"—even men who grow up gay. I always presumed that many of the younger gay men who came to The Pose Workshop—whether "out" or not—already had vivid memories of seeing both female models in "men's sophisticates" and male models in various gay men's magazines. Did The Pose Workshop experience change how gay male participants looked at such pictures of men? Perhaps, although I cannot say with any certainty. I suspect that to find out, participants in a discussion would have to include primarily gay- or bi-identified men.

The question of male models came up quite often in discussion, among people of all sexual orientations; and I tried to find a way to clarify, for people unfamiliar with magazines marketed to gay men, that there do exist pictures in which the male model's pose and affect closely resemble female models' self-abnegation in standard heterosexual men's magazines, like the ones the group was just looking at. Such pictures are not hard to find, I explained, in shops catering primarily to gay men: The male model looks young and drugged, for instance, his anus may be prominently displayed to the camera, and he looks decidedly vulnerable and diminished. It would probably be difficult, in fact, to find a pose in a heterosexual men's magazine that has not been matched quite closely by a male model in a gay men's magazine somewhere. Sexual subordination does not have a gender, I frequently pointed out. But far more typical are pictures in which the male model is posed as an embodiment of boundaried self-possession and exemplary bodily integrity: His body is abundantly strong and muscled, his facial expression is his own, and his eyes are alert. This is generally true not only of explicitly gay male magazines but also of *Playgirl*-type magazines. The photographic illusion is maintained that the man is *there,* that his sexual agency and persona have not been compromised or "disappeared" in order to make his image more arousing. He appears actively present, even if he is shown prepared to be entered. And typically, in a series of photos where a particular male model's rectum *is* on display and available, there are subsequent photos where he is shown with his "body integrity" back (literally, for instance, he is shown with an erection ready to penetrate or he is shown manually masturbating himself). Typically in "heterosexual" photography, by contrast, once the female model's personality and bodily integrity have been annulled, that's the end—and that's who she ever "is."

Once, at a conference, I was informed by a workshop participant that after he had posed, a man from among the spectators —apparently smitten with him during the exercise—followed him around after the workshop and sexually harassed him. That, I learned, was another downside of The Pose Workshop, one I could not possibly avert with certainty.

❖

I selected most photos from mainstream, newsstand magazines, but I generally added a few from magazines that could be purchased only in an "adult" bookstore—one, for instance, consisted entirely of pictures of a Caucasian woman tied and bound to a bench with a ball gag in her mouth. In the marketplace at large, the women in magazines for sale to men tend to be Caucasian, so in selecting pictures of women who are "nonwhite," I deliberately sought representative materials portraying the model's race with a specific sexual connotation not incidental to the pose. For instance, one of the magazines I used shows various poses of an African-American woman at least eight months pregnant; it is called *Black Mama*. As in much pornography showing people of color, consumers' attention is drawn to the model's racial traits, which are sexualized and commoditized. (To my repeated amazement, Caucasian male posers who replicated a photo from this magazine rarely ever noticed, until told later, that the model is pregnant. Perhaps once they perceived "black," that was all they saw.) Another magazine I used shows infantilized Asian women who are dressed to appear underage but who are identified on the cover as being eighteen; their breasts are relatively small and their pubic hair has been shaved.

I believed it important that my selection of magazines represent at least some of the racism peddled by the pornography industry, even if this point was never brought up during discussion. I wanted to convey to workshop participants, at least at a subconscious level, the connection between what happens to women in these photos *as women* and what happens to women of color in addition. Whatever got said out loud about the racial meaning of the pictures depended almost entirely, of course, upon who the workshop participants were. Not surprisingly, this racial dynamic often went unremarked in all-"white" groups; so I would call attention to it, at least in passing. But if the workshop consisted predominantly or partly of people of color, such prompting was rarely necessary, because in truth there is no way not to see—and say—how "race" is part of what makes *all* the pictures "sexy."

As exercise leader I always had some latitude to decide—although very quickly—which of the randomly selected posers got which picture. If the workshop group was racially mixed, I was careful to make certain that the distribution of pictures to posers did not send an unintended message. For instance, if two of the pictures were of women of color and two of the posers happened to be men of color, I avoided pairing those particular posers and pictures—which might have sent an unintended and indecipherable signal to workshop participants. In my experience as someone of Northern European ancestry conducting racially mixed workshops in the United States, I generally made sure that men of color were given a picture of a "white" woman to pose and pictures of women of color were given to "white" men.

I can imagine circumstances in which the pose-exercise leader is himself a person of color and participants are also predominantly people of color, and then, perhaps, it may be appropriate to use photographs from magazines targeted to a racially defined market of heterosexual men (as *Players* and *Black Tail* are for African-American men). But even then, I imagine, the majority of the photographs should be of "white" women, in order not to obscure the white-supremacist "beauty" standards particular to the US pornography industry.

I had many occasions to observe the issue of race as it was raised by participants themselves during discussion—sometimes, it seemed, without participants' conscious knowledge. For instance, I frequently heard men say, in words more or less the same, "I don't see any problem—she got paid for it." Typically, such men went on to relate some "facts" they had read—usually in this very sort of magazine—about how much women can get paid for posing for photographers this way. What was remarkable was that, in ten years, I heard this said only by men who are "white." In racially mixed groups, I do not recall ever hearing a man of color make such a comment. I listened silently to all such intellectual defenses of men's pornography consumption, of course; my job as discussion leader was to elicit feelings, not rebut. But I pondered this particular smoke screen more than all the others that wafted in. *Is it possible,* I wondered, *that for men of color in the United States, witnessing someone doing something that is obviously*

degrading, the rationalization "She got paid for it" is simply less cred-
ible than it is for men who—because they were born "white" into
white supremacy—may not have been so historically sensitized to
demeaning and alienated labor?

I do not know the answer; nor can I, of course. It's just a thought—a question prompted in my mind from hearing thousands of men of all colors talk about how it felt to pose and how it felt to watch.

❖

After conducting approximately six poses, I would do another count-off to form discussion groups. The method was really simple: If there were a total of forty people in the workshop and I wanted four groups, each with a facilitator, I asked everyone to count off by four. First I counted off the posers, to make sure there would be at least one poser in each discussion group; then I said, "Now, I'm going to ask you all to count off by 4s [or however many small groups I wanted to form]. Remember your number." For the first time I introduced the other workshop cofacilitators by name, then I directed the counted-off small groups to specific locations ("Number 1s go over there with Tom. Number 2s go with Dick," and so forth). Five to ten people per group worked best.

If one of the posers presented a serious problem during the pose exercise (because, for instance, he "pandered" or he experienced some acute and personal emotional distress), I made sure he was not alone as the only poser in a small group.

The original members of MAP and I experimented with many

different ideas about how best to facilitate discussions after the posing exercise. Through much trial and error, here's what we found worked best.

Ground rules. For two or three minutes at the beginning, each discussion leader would say his name and a brief self-introduction, then propose some ground rules (for everyone's sense of safety) and ask that everyone in the group agree to them:

- "Everything each person says here is confidential and will not be repeated outside this room with anyone's name attached."
- "Each person will have time to speak in turn."
- "Each person agrees to speak as honestly as they can from their own experience and feelings, and not object to or criticize what someone else has said."
- "Each person agrees not to refer to what someone else has said without first asking that person's permission."
- "Each person agrees to listen to everyone else with complete respect and without interrupting, no matter what is said."

To some, these ground rules may not seem terribly significant (and to others they may be arguable politically); but in my experience, they did something absolutely necessary: They reestablished for workshop participants a social zone of personal integrity and individual responsibility—assumptions that had been seriously disrupted during the pose exercise as one person after another had their line of consent crossed. Hearing everyone agree to these ground rules began to reaffirm, for each individual, the possibility of speaking in a personal voice that would be heard. I never commented on the dynamics of this process; I just made sure it started to happen—by asking for the group's collective and active assent: "Can we all agree on these ground rules?"

When I conducted the pose exercise and also facilitated the discussion, these ground rules had an additional function: They helped me make a humanizing transition—both in myself and in the eyes of the group—from having just cavalierly ordered people around. By this respectful act of proposing ground rules, I could begin to relocate and restore certain everyday ethical obligations that I had necessarily suspended in order to conduct the poses. Thus this moment at the beginning of the discussion period was always a great personal relief.

The first go-round. Next, I asked people in the group to introduce themselves, going around the circle one by one, and to do so I asked them to answer some version of this simple, straightforward question:

- "What is one thing you have done in your life to act against sexism or to be an ally of women?"

Workshop participants always seemed somewhat surprised when I began our discussion with that question, or some paraphrase, because it had absolutely nothing to do with the exercise they'd just been through. I asked people for a brief, personal answer: "No résumés and no one-upmanship, please." I asked people to say whatever came into their minds, however slight it seemed. "And," I emphasized, "there are no right or wrong answers. Just name one thing."

This first go-round question was remarkably effective. It not only began self-disclosure on a very positive, affirming note; it was also—consistent with The Pose Workshop's unique experiential method—usefully disconcerting. By the time many people came through the pose exercise, especially many men, their affect and demeanor often seemed downcast. They had just been *watching* stuff and *doing* stuff that might well have made them feel very low self-worth. And the first thing they were asked to answer was, in effect, "What's a pride point in your life?" For many participants, responding to this question appeared to be mental work; many struggled to think of *anything* that could qualify, even remotely, as "an act against sexism or to be an ally of women." But pitching this question to the group was a key step in The Pose Workshop process. For men especially it sent the subtextual message that "somewhere in your life you made at least one choice that was very worthwhile, and you should be proud of making that choice; you made it, and you did it." As facilitator, I found I needed only to encourage people, to draw out their responses, assuring them that even the slightest thing they did was appropriate to say.

The first go-ground went relatively quickly, no more than two or three minutes per person. If someone talked on and on, I'd gently interrupt and appeal to the need for everyone to have enough time to speak. People at times were shy; they sometimes also tended to copy one another. If one person started out by saying, "Well, I try to be a good example to my daughter," for instance, several other daughter stories might follow. I always let it be. I trusted that the workshop's unique method functioned at a hidden, interior level—in the private mental work people did in order to answer the question at all—rather than out loud in the literal content of the answers people spoke.

I remember giving The Pose Workshop at an all-male college, for residence advisers and various other student leaders. When I asked the first go-round question, "Name one thing you have done in your life to be an ally of women," the first man started talking about the fact that a woman friend had been raped, and he told how he tried to be supportive to her, to help her through it by listening and being there for her. Then the second man spoke and told a similar story: "A friend of mine was being battered by her boyfriend and I tried to talk to her, to support her, to help her get out of the relationship." Slowly but surely the question worked its way around this all-male group at this all-male school, and by the end of the go-round most men had related a first-person story about having been told by a woman friend some incident of sexual assault she had experienced. To my knowledge, none of these undergrads had ever shared such stories before. But suddenly there was a roomful of them—stories that are commonplace among many college-age people today but rarely shared conscientiously by men in conversation.

Many more men now in their twenties have heard such stories from women friends than have men a generation or more older. The vocabulary of acquaintance rape, battery, stalking, and sexual harassment is relatively recent. Today, especially on campuses, women draw not only women friends but selected men friends into their confidence, sometimes to tell of experiencing sexual violence in the new shared language that now exists to name it. As a result, many younger men today carry such stories very near their heart, though they do not have any idea how many *other* men have personally been told how many *other* stories of sexual violence against particular women. On occasion, The Pose Workshop functioned to break down that wall of silence.

The second go-round. Only after everyone had a chance to introduce themselves did I bring the subject around to the exercise everyone just experienced: "Now we're each going to have a chance to talk about how it felt to do the pose and how it felt to watch." I always asked the poser or posers in the group to speak first: "How did it feel to pose?" Sometimes, to draw them out, I would repeat the question—especially before each poser spoke— and ask more specific and detailed questions along the same line, such as "How did it feel when people were calling out directions to you? How did it feel when you were watching someone else pose and you knew you'd be next?" Listening to posers describe how they felt posing tended to be riveting for everyone in the discussion—not least because some group members were still feeling relief that they were not picked to pose.

For me personally, hearing a poser speak was always of interest in another way. Whenever I conducted the pose exercise, I could never remember who did which pose. It was some sort of mental blockage: My focus was on so many other things that the individual poser tended to become invisible to me as a distinct personality. Or perhaps this was a trick my conscience played on me: It went "on hold" so that I could put the poser through his paces without conflict—without regarding him as "real." That was almost always what happened; I don't know why. Only when a poser started talking in his real voice did he become recognizable to me, as a personality, in the discussion group. So as I began each discussion, I found I had to ask all the posers in the circle to identify themselves, and which pose they did as well. This mental blockage never went away with practice; in fact, the more years I conducted The Pose Workshop, the more pronounced it became. Perhaps this recurring mental lapse was trying to tell me something: Getting people to "do the pose" participates to some extent in the same ethics of disrespect used in the production of pornography. *Perhaps,* I sometimes mused, *the educational end of The Pose Workshop does not justify its experiential means.*

It was important for people to hear the posers first, so I drew them out patiently and personally. Then and only then did I ask spectators to speak, one at a time, going around the circle: "How did it feel to watch?" When a poser's turn came, I asked him to speak again, but as a spectator this time, repeating the question like a mantra: "How did it feel to watch these men posing?"

If people seemed unable to think of anything to say, I used additional questions to draw them out: "How did it feel to call out comments? How did it feel to look back and forth between the picture in the magazine and the man doing the pose? How did you feel about the other spectators' comments and reactions?" but always returning to the same basic question: "How did it feel to watch?"

People in the discussion circle still did not know what was going on. They didn't know where it was headed; they didn't know why they'd done the pose exercise; they didn't know why they were being asked these questions. The Pose Workshop deliberately disarmed expectations of all sorts, revealing no cogency, no "intellectual" content, until the very last minute. Along the way, therefore, some participants seized occasions to impose their own.

I developed my own methods for subtly keeping discussions on track, to steer people's responses away from debates, ideological grandstanding, rhetorical riffs, and so forth. Such diversions obviously indicated to me that the respondent was resisting, with all his mental might, talking about feelings open-endedly without any clear-cut intellectual purpose. But I knew that to argue with such flim-flam or to rebut it—or even to comment on it substantively—would simply aid and abet the respondent's digging in behind a defensive mental barricade. I learned that the following techniques always worked much better:

- If a respondent used the word "pornography," I kept referring to "the pictures we saw," "pictures in magazines like that"—to keep perceptions focused on the specific, not a projection or abstraction.
- I kept reminding people to speak from their feelings ("as we all agreed at the beginning that's what we wanted to do").
- I gave positive recognition to statements that expressed feelings, "underlining" something said, for instance, by paraphrasing it for emphasis and restating it. This repetition not only helped the respondent feel heard; this often helped other people in the group hear the feeling—and offered the respondent a needed sense of permission to say more.
- I listened actively, trying to be the most exemplary listener in the circle. I viewed my facilitator job as mostly concentrating completely on what someone was saying, thus setting an important tone for the rest of the people in the group, and thus averting a "devil's advocate" or

"debating society" atmosphere. I tended to look intently into the eyes of the person who was speaking, I often nodded, and I often murmured "uh-huh" to keep participants talking. I judiciously asked leading questions until I got the sense that the respondent had finished saying whatever they could say. Mentally, I kept reminding myself that nothing is boring, nothing is "wrong." The point was not to elicit any particular "right" answers; the point was to keep people focused, in their own private mind, on the basic question ("How did it feel to watch?").

- I kept the circular structure of the go-round visible, so that participants could expect to have their own turn to talk personally. If I got restless, that would only feed people's impatience, making it more likely that someone would erupt with a polemic digression. Instead, I visualized everyone meditating on the go-round question—perhaps somewhere deep inside, beyond where I or anyone else could perceive.

- I deliberately allowed interpretive vocabulary to come from participants' own report of their experience. I tried never to interpose subjective words before a participant had mentioned them first. Then, when such a word had been introduced by someone to name their experience, I used it in paraphrasing and "underlining." I mentally stored up the interpretive language that came out of people's own mouths. I heard such words as "vulnerable," "humiliating," "degrading," "uncomfortable" quite commonly. One man in a workshop said, "I felt like a side of beef hanging up in a slaughterhouse." I listened intently for the metaphors, the images, the exact words that came from people talking about how it felt to pose or how it felt to watch. I kept asking the "How did it feel . . . ?" questions and absorbed like a sponge whatever was said. Then I could refer back to people's stated experience, in language that actually named the experience meaningfully because the words came from participants themselves.

- I stayed prepared for, and accepting of, a wide range of emotional discharge. People might shake, weep, laugh, and so forth. Always I assumed that there might be sexual-abuse survivors present who might never identify themselves. Always I assumed that for some survivors of sexual abuse, these pictures might have triggered memories—perhaps because such pictures were known by the survivor to have been used by her or his perpetrator. Also, always I assumed that even if a group looked homogeneous, it was not. For the generality of young men in the United States, for instance, the magazines used in The Pose Workshop would be very familiar—some recent issues used, perhaps, as aids to masturbation—yet there might be exceptions. Generally speaking, the pictures would not be so indelibly recollected by women; yet there might be exceptions. And some participants would be seeing such photos for the first time. I recall facilitating a discussion among university students when it turned out some were women who had recently moved to the United States from a country where such photography is not publicly displayed—and they were traumatized.

- I steered away from speculation about the actual circumstances that produced the pictures. The Pose Workshop did not purport to replicate a photo shoot, and never was any factual information presented about what did or did not actually take place when the "pose" pictures were taken. Nevertheless, discussants would sometimes veer away from the discussion to offer received opinions about photo sessions, professional modeling, going pay rates, and so forth; so I would refocus attention on the picture, the pose, participants' own feelings, and participants' own perceptions.

- I also steered discussion away from speculative myths about gender. I often heard women acknowledge during discussions that the poses—clichés of sexualized "femininity" par excellence—were very familiar; and women often remarked, with bemusement, about how the men had to struggle to "do the pose," whereas for women they'd be a snap. This was always a useful and telling point about sex-role socialization—not to be confused with its "Biology is destiny" version, however: Occasionally a man or a woman would put forth the view that female anatomy is "naturally" suited for such poses but men's bodies aren't, therefore the premise of the exercise is bunk. I never argued; I didn't even mention what patent nonsense this was; I just pulled the focus back to people's real feelings in the moment.

- I steered away from pronouncements about particular

participants' sexual relationship to the pictures. I assumed there was *some* sexual arousal in the group during the pose exercise—from looking at the pictures and/or from looking at the men in the poses—but I never expected anyone to say so. I talked *as if* these pictures were similar to pictures some people in the group might have masturbated to, but I did not call personal attention to anyone in particular. If a participant tried to opt out of answering a go-round question by declaring (as if scoring brownie points) that he was "not turned on by pictures like this," I would simply restate the question straightforwardly ("Yes, but how did it feel to pose—to watch?") and clarify that I was not necessarily asking about *sexual* feelings.

The third go-round. During the first go-round I allotted two to three minutes per person; during the second go-round, three to four minutes per person. But the third go-round, the last, moved *very* quickly:

- "What were those pictures *of?*"

This question always elicited a pile-up of reactions, perhaps more intriguing in sum than separately. I sometimes elaborated, encouraging people to give quick, off-the-top-of-their-head answers: "Describe those pictures, with the first words that come into your head. There's no right or wrong answer. Just what did you *see?* What were those pictures *of?*" The purpose was to prompt people to reflect on their own powers of observation, their perceptual faculties. *The answers to the question didn't matter*—but participants never knew this. The point was to get people to answer *something*. To answer the question at all, they had to have made some re-adjustment inside their own brain; they had to have become observant of their own perceptual process. That was a subtext of go-round questions #1 and #2, but it was key to #3. So long as the answer responded to the question "What are those pictures *of?*"—so long as the response was even approximately on point—there was no answer that was better and no answer that was worse.

A key to The Pose Workshop was built into this question: Answering it brought to consciousness a process that had been set in motion at the start of the exercise—the experience of recognizing one's capacity to perceive these pictures differently. That process was given a boost during discussion, when participants were led to reflect personally ("What was I doing there? What was I feeling there? Who was *I* in relationship to what I saw and what I did? What's going on in me?"). That process was the subtextual purpose of answering "How did it feel to pose? How did it feel to watch? How did it feel to call out instructions to the posers?" And finally, answering "What are those pictures *of?*" brought into sharper focus how it felt to be in a particular power relationship to another person—like a camera, like a camera operator—just *looking*. Whatever people answered, they might also be mentally processing something of what *other* people in the circle already answered—perhaps comments about feeling vulnerable, powerless, accessible, uncomfortable, put down. Whatever people answered, they might also be mentally processing the fact that they now thought about the person in the photo as more real than before. Thus, being on the spot and having to answer the question "What are those pictures *of?*" necessarily stirred up a sea-change inside. The quite cryptic question asked people to give a name to what they saw. The *name they gave* didn't matter. Affirming their own capacity to *perceive* was the point. This third go-round had a cumulative effect, because people were not only reflecting on their own seeing; people were hearing words for what *other* people were seeing. People blurted out words and saw themselves seeing. Some people said "naked women." Some people said "pieces of meat." Some people said "humiliation, objectification." Some people said "sex." It was always a remarkable moment; people often made astonishing free associations. And like the tip of an iceberg that had drifted to the tropics, each enunciation portended a submerged, internal thaw.

The wrap-up. After everyone in the circle had briefly answered the question about what the pictures are *of,* I took three to five minutes to speak to the group personally and informally to conclude The Pose Workshop experience. Referring back to things participants said, I used the interpretive language that emerged from their own perceptions. I never followed a script exactly, but I tried to make sure that I touched on the following main point, intentionally personally empowering:

- "You just saw with your own eyes. The way you looked at these pictures today was to use your own eyes. What you saw, you saw for yourself. These might be new eyes, just opened for the first time here today. But they're *your* eyes, and you can look through them again."

It seemed to surprise many people when I said that. Perhaps knowing that I cofounded a group called Men Against

Pornography, many people assumed The Pose Workshop was headed in a very hard-line, doctrinal direction ("Now here's what you're supposed to think . . ."). But such closure never came. Instead, I went on ad-libbing, casually saying things like these:

- "You're probably wondering about the purpose of that exercise—where a man did the pose in a picture. It might have looked goofy and gooney and awkward; it might have been a laugh at first. It might also have made you wonder how anyone could really be having a good time posing like that. And looking back and forth between the picture and the guy posing—well, maybe you saw something about the picture that you hadn't seen before. Maybe that picture looks different to you now, after you've seen a man struggling into the pose. Maybe the picture also looks *the same* as before. You can look at it both ways. You can look at the picture the old way *and* you can see it the new way."

- "If you recall only one thing from this workshop, remember that you have two sets of eyes. You have a way of perceiving where you suspend your belief in the reality of that other person, perhaps in order to feel sexually turned on. You also have a way of perceiving where you can see that what is happening to somebody in that picture is happening to someone who is as real as you are."

- "If you have masturbated to pictures like this, there's really no point in slapping your wrist and saying no-no-no. To those of you who've masturbated to pictures like this, I offer this idea: If you masturbate to the pictures at night, take them out in the light of day the next morning—and look at them with the 'new eyes' you found in this workshop."

Such an informal wrap-up helped name the very experience that many men in the room just had. It came at the point when their new recognition had dawned, and it underscored that these "new eyes" were their own. Having briefly inhabited the model's discomfort, many men had now extrapolated that her languid face could not possibly reflect what's going on in the rest of her; many men had privately noted what a put-on they'd been duped by, what a ruse had aroused them. And they had begun to notice that they were themselves in a loop of manipulation and self-deception: To feel turned on, they misread their own senses; they believed a phony photo instead. The very photo that put her *down* also put him *on*. As facilitator I had no need to say all this, because each participant's experience already spoke private volumes. The workshop itself helped decode the picture, helped dislodge and sort out two very different ways of seeing. I never told participants what to see or how to see it. They saw on their own, with their own "new eyes."

I figure approximately eighty percent of male workshop participants had an experience that stayed with them. That doesn't necessarily mean they stopped using pornography, but it means they realized they had a way of looking at the pictures differently. And that's a big step. For a man who experiences himself as powerless to diminish his own pornography consumption, powerless to diminish its effect on his erotic intimacy with a lover—if his sexual buttons seem "automatically" pushed every time he looks at it—learning to see with "new eyes" can be a new and empowering beginning: a possibility in himself he did not know was there, a chance to relearn his reality by learning to perceive another's. Once he has seen through his "new eyes," he can decide whether to perceive through them ever again. It's his choice—always a choice, and always his.

❖

In ten years of conducting The Pose Workshop, I have observed thousands of men looking at how they look at "sexy" photographs, and I have listened as they opened up to speak their feelings—not their theories or opinions—in an experience that helped them perceive pornography as documenting *something happening to someone real,* someone who is as real as themselves. Over the years, certain responses recurred with regularity: "I felt vulnerable . . . awkward . . . humiliated . . . uncomfortable . . . embarrassed . . . degraded." "I didn't feel sexy at all." "I didn't feel turned on at all." Other personal responses were even more graphic and specific.

Typically and simultaneously, there were also opinionated responses that appeared to be not feelings so much as attempts to mentally process the feelings away, such as: "She was paid to do that. I don't see any problem. I'd do it too if I was paid."

I frequently heard comments from participants that revealed a significant shift in perception: "I was glad I didn't have to pose; he looked really uncomfortable." "At first I enjoyed calling out comments, but then it got really heavy and I felt awful for calling out anything." "At first I thought it was going to be fun, but once I really got into doing the pose I realized something else was going on." "Looking at a guy doing the pose made me see just how ridiculous those pictures are." Many men also volunteered something at the end about how they expected the workshop to affect them in the future: "I don't think I'll be able to look at those pictures the same way again."

The Pose Workshop was set up so that no individual man's sexual history in relationship to such pictures was ever judged; he was never made to feel shame or blame. Quite the contrary, he was encouraged to "look at the pictures with new eyes; see what those pictures are really *of*." Young men were often shocked when I disclosed the stack of magazines from which "pose" photographs had been selected, though not because they had never seen such a collection before. Today *Playboy, Penthouse,* and other such magazines are a fixture of sex education for young men, who are commonly introduced to them by peers, by their fathers, or by other men their father's age. I was a witness during The Pose Workshop, however, as many young men became aware that they were looking at these familiar magazines in a new way—and they were genuinely amazed.

Men's individual consumption of magazines such as *Playboy* and *Penthouse*—as purchasers, as browsers, and as users during private episodes of masturbation—is apparently very dependent upon looking at such pictures as if the women in the photographs are less real than the men's sexual feelings. From repetitive personal experience—reinforced by the sensation of ejaculatory release— men learn that if what they desire is erotic stimulation from such published pictorials (to feel "turned on to pornography like a real man") they had better not perceive or conceive of the pictured women as being equally real people. For many men "hooked" on pornography, such pictures do not "work" as a turn-on if the

73

woman is regarded as a real person. This, it turns out, is what makes pornography "sexy." And this dissociative way of looking seems also to result in dissociative feeling: conditioned to shut off or numb out in a relational context of actual intimacy and equality.

Conversely, when a man, even momentarily, looks at a pictured woman as if she is as real as himself—as if what is happening to her (in the photograph) is real and as if her feelings are real too—the photograph may lose its perceptual distance and hence its effectiveness as an erotic stimulus. This experience is self-evidently far more to be desired than dreaded, as The Pose Workshop may prepare a man to realize. As he does so, he may find himself on the brink of a profound new personal discovery, with implications for all his relational life: He may learn not only to fully perceive the person he has feelings for but also to perceive that person as someone who need be no less real than he in order for him to feel.

PORNOGRAPHY SELF-CHECK *

My Past

- ❑ I can remember learning a lot about what sex is supposed to be from pornography.
- ❑ I can remember looking at pornography with other boys.
- ❑ I can remember pornography my father used.
- ❑ I can remember using pornography to feel OK about myself.
- ❑ I can remember comparing some of the girls and women I met to the women's bodies I saw in pornography.
- ❑ I can remember comparing myself to the men in pornography.
- ❑ I can remember thinking I should keep my relation to pornography a secret.
- ❑ I can remember times when I felt an almost overwhelming need for certain pornography.

My Present

- ❑ I sometimes privately remember pornography I've used while I'm having sex with someone.
- ❑ I sometimes compare my sex partner to the people's bodies I've seen in pornography.
- ❑ I sometimes can't masturbate unless I use pornography.
- ❑ I sometimes am afraid my sexual performance will not be as masculine as the men who perform in pornography.

❑ I sometimes can't perform sexually unless I'm thinking about pornography.

❑ I sometimes find myself staring at someone's body or a body part because it reminds me of something I've seen in pornography.

❑ I sometimes can't feel turned on without pornography.

❑ I sometimes use pornography to masturbate when I feel . . .
  ❑ Tense ❑ Lonely ❑ Restless ❑ Withdrawn ❑ Angry ❑ Worthless ❑ Odd

❑ I sometimes use pornography to masturbate when I feel . . .
  ❑ Outgoing ❑ Well-liked ❑ Proud ❑ Happy ❑ Confident ❑ In love ❑ Self-worth

❑ I sometimes prefer having sex with pornography to having sex with another person.

❑ I sometimes have the feeling during a sexual experience that I'm not really *there* with anyone—it's as if I'm in a private world just getting off.

❑ I sometimes don't feel any better about myself after using pornography than before.

❑ I sometimes feel withdrawn or irritable with my sexual partner after I've privately used pornography.

❑ I sometimes can't stop my mind from thinking about pornography while I'm having sex with someone.

❑ I sometimes wonder if my sexual feelings have been permanently affected by pornography.

- ❏ I would like my sexual feelings to be honest ones.
- ❏ I would like to be free from comparing my sexuality or my partner's to pornography.
- ❏ I would like to experience affection and intimacy without using pornography to fake it.
- ❏ I would like to really *be with* my partner during sex— without disappearing, without pretending, and without needing pornography to feel my feelings.
- ❏ I would like to_____

JOHN STOLTENBERG is the acclaimed author of *Refusing to Be a Man: Essays on Sex and Justice* (Meridian, 1990), a revolutionary examination of male sexual identity that has been adopted in hundreds of courses—in gender studies, philosophy, religion, psychology, sociology, law, and political science. His second book, *The End of Manhood: A Book for Men of Conscience* (Plume, 1993), is a practical guide to everyday relationships—how to live as a man of conscience in love, in sex, in families, among friends. "Stoltenberg's new male," said the *New York Times Book Review*, "is able to reach beyond gender differences into the humanizing depths of everyone's gender-free soul."

Stoltenberg is cofounder of Men Against Pornography and a frequent speaker and workshop leader at colleges and conferences. He has taught at the New School for Social Research and has appeared on hundreds of radio and television programs. He holds a master of divinity degree from Union Theological Seminary in New York City and a master of fine arts in theater from Columbia University School of the Arts.

More from the Milkweed Editions Thistle series: